DON'T LET THEM TELL YOU HOW TO GRIEVE

Bereavement:
Lines to let you know
you're not alone

About the author

Gina Claye is a retired teacher, living in the Chiltern hills. Her poems for children have been published in anthologies by *Scholastic* and *Oxford University Press*. She has helped counsel parents who have lost a child, and advised hospital staff on the needs of those grieving, drawing on her personal experiences. She has appeared on television and radio.

She can be contacted via her website at
www.ginaclaye.co.uk

DON'T LET THEM TELL YOU HOW TO GRIEVE

Bereavement:
Lines to let you know
you're not alone

by

Gina Claye

Gina Claye

OxPen

First published in Great Britain 2006 for OxPen by WritersPrintShop

ISBN 1904623441

Designed by e-BookServices.com
Cover Image by Rachael Oilfield

www.ginaclaye.co.uk
www.writersservices.com/wbs/books/ginaclaye.htm

Acknowledgements

Thanks to my daughter, Rachael, for editing this book, for making many valuable suggestions, for hearing me out with love and even occasional patience, and for her belief in this project; also for giving me a lovely granddaughter, Nancy. I should like to thank members of Oxford Writers' Group for their support, and in particular, Linora Lawrence, who read the manuscript, made suggestions, and encouraged me each step of the way. Also to Chas Jones of WritersServices for his advice.

Thanks also to Judy G, my support worker from Cruse Bereavement Care, for her kindness and her listening ear. It was in a Christmas card to her that I first wrote a short poem, 'Grief', and she encouraged me to write the rest of the collection. Thanks also to The Compassionate Friends (TCF), an organisation for bereaved families that put me in touch with other grieving mums and dads after my daughter Nikki died.

Remembering David Gillett for his love and support, and thanks to Bill for his kindness and cooking. Also to Tim and Ann for battling with bureaucracy. And to my mum, my late dad, and my sister Ruth and her family, who, in the face of their own grief, have supported me and shown me great love.

to

Nikki and Robin

and

Rachael, Emma and Lucy,
three strong women

and

to all who grieve

Cruse Bereavement Care

Cruse Bereavement Care exists to promote the well-being of bereaved people and to enable anyone bereaved by death to understand their grief and cope with their loss. The organisation provides counselling and support. It offers information, advice, education and training services.

Day by Day helpline 0870 167 1677
www.crusebereavementcare.org.uk
helpline@crusebereavementcare.org.uk

The Compassionate Friends

The Compassionate Friends (TCF) is an organisation of bereaved parents and their families, offering understanding, support and encouragement to others after the death of a child or children. They also offer support, advice and information to other relatives, friends and professionals who are helping the family.

TCF National Office, Tel 0845 120 3785
Helpline 0845 1232304
www.tcf.org.uk
info@tcf.org.uk

USA www.compassionatefriends.org

Australia www.compassionatefriendsvictoria.org.au

The Poems

Foreword

In 1987 my elder daughter, Nikki, aged 19, took her own life. Just over a year later, my husband left. For a marriage to survive the death of a child is hard enough; it is less likely to survive if that death is a suicide. When he left, out of the blue, it felt like another bereavement. During the next three years I had even more adjustments to make; my son left home to go to university, I had to train to become a teacher as I now had to earn my own living, my younger daughter left home, and finally, I had to sell the house and find somewhere else to live.

Then in 2003, Robin, aged 32, my son and close friend after all we had been through, fell ill in Singapore and died suddenly a few days later, of encephalitis. We were all devastated. I had lost two of my three children and my younger daughter, Rachael, had lost both her siblings. It was during the two years after Robin's death that I wrote these poems. I could not have written them if I had not already gone through the grief of Nikki's death. This time, although it was just as painful, I was able to observe and identify my thoughts and feelings. The poems helped me not only to come to terms with my own grief, but to create something positive out of the lives and deaths of my two children.

Not long after my daughter Nikki's death, I met a woman whose family believed that after two years she ought to be 'over it by now'. She wanted to cry over her son's jacket, but felt she shouldn't after all that time. I felt that she should follow her instinct, and not hold back. It seems to me that grief is a long process and we deal with it in different ways, and that we should allow others to grieve in their own way in their own time, and ask them to let us do the same.

Don't let them tell you how to grieve

Don't let them tell you how to grieve.
Though it's the same journey for all
there is no one way through.
Others may do it differently.
Let them. If you don't like
what they're saying, get them to leave.
Don't let them tell you how to grieve.

So what if your house is a mess.
Leave it. Tomorrow you just might
need to wring hell out of a dishcloth
or beat up a rug or two.
Never mind any raised eyebrows,
go by how you feel.
Don't let them tell you how to grieve.

Sit in the garden for hours drinking tea.
Dead head one rose.
Talk to the weeds if you want to.
Tell them it's their turn tomorrow,
whenever that is.
Let the grass grow under your feet.
Don't let them tell you how to grieve.

Don't do a big shop-up just
because you ought to. Order a pizza,
or heat up one of the unknown
objects lurking in the freezer.

Hug a bowl of custard. Have tomatoes
on toast for breakfast, lunch and tea.
Don't let them tell you how to grieve.

Ignore advice to pull yourself together.
Sit in the dark or light a candle.
It's OK to cry, to remember.
Wear his old sweater; let it hug you.
Sob over his jacket if it's what you need.
Sink a brandy, or two, or three.
Don't let them tell you how to grieve.

Refuse that kindly meant invitation
to get you out again.
If you don't want to go, say so.
Friends may mutter, shake their heads.
Don't take any notice. Let them.
They don't know exactly how you feel.
They're not the ones who've been bereaved.
Don't let them tell you how to grieve.

At first I had this very strong feeling that life was over. It all seemed pointless.

Yesterday

Yesterday
        we shared a meal,
                opened a bottle

of wine, filled our days
        together. Today I
                cook for one

for something to do, scrape
        much of it into the bin
                uneaten. And tomorrow,

I have no plans for tomorrow.
        Tell me, what
                am I to do

with this leftover life?

On both occasions after my children died, the house filled up. There were people in the kitchen making cups of tea; some sat out on the patio, while others chatted in the sitting room, often until late into the night.

Talk

It is comforting to have
others about, as long as
they talk amongst themselves

and not to me. It's hard enough
to take in what they're saying
and too much effort

to speak, let alone think
of an answer. But they have
others at home waiting.

And I dread it when they go
and the house is empty
and I am alone.

It was a profound consolation to read the words of love and support I received – I don't think I could have kept going without them. One very simple piece of advice was given to me by someone I hadn't known long but who has since become a dear friend. They were exactly what I needed to hear at that point and they have helped me ever since.

Words

For Lucy

Words come in different forms,
printed on cards, confined
to a sympathy space with edges,
a name with love underneath.

Or written on a blank sheet
with a black pen,
their owner wondering if one
will bring comfort.

Some come in quotations,
typed or copperplate,
they counsel courage and calm
which I don't have, not now.

Others materialise down the phone,
'Don't take decisions for at least a year.'
They speak of experience,
a soul's similar dilemma.

Kind words from kind friends,
and they help. Whatever
form, they all help,
I will not say heal,

those bold lines
hang in the future,
not on my wall,
not now.

But the words I cling to
are Lucy's words, simple
and circled with a hug
on which everyday I lean.

'One foot in front of the other
and don't forget to breathe.'

I seemed to be living life in a dream; normal everyday routine had come to an abrupt halt. I have a vivid memory of cards and flowers everywhere and neighbours popping home to get more vases.

Filling up

Cards on every surface,
flowers in the sink,
letters absently placed
on top of an empty fridge.

How would I manage
without the love shown by all?
The phone rings each minute,
the doorbell interrupts each call.

But especially welcome
to this bereaved household
is the friend who also brings
a **large** casserole.

I had the strange experience at times that the ground was giving way under my feet. I suppose it is an example of how the mind, or perhaps a strong emotion such as grief, can affect us physically. All I know is that this sensation of not walking on firm ground was very real.

Freefall

I'm free falling,
tumbling,
no point is
fixed. If
there is a future
without you,
it will be paced out
by the passing kindnesses,
half grasped, half
unwanted,
in the hours, days that
slide around
me, until finally,
finally
I stop.

My house is not far from the centre of town, and as I walked up to buy essentials, I would see people clutching towels on their way to the swimming pool, popping into the bank or returning videos. They were going about their usual daily lives, something I was sure I would never be able to do again.

Isolation

Life's not real
anymore
though it's going on around me
as before.

Separated from everyone by
an invisible wall,
I'm not taking part in it
at all.

Robin had bought a house in Norwich which had been let to students while he and his partner, Emma, were in Singapore. Although my ex-husband had dealt with financial matters initially, he was living at the time in Nigeria, and so I found myself undertaking the task. The mortgage company, though requested not to, kept addressing letters in Robin's name which I found extremely upsetting. The pile of letters mounted up and I had to steel myself to look at them. I was in no mind to think clearly.

Bureaucracy

I've filled in yet another
important form. Put it somewhere.
Can't find it.

Searched for it everywhere,
in the dustbin, in the wardrobe,
even in the piles of paper

waiting to be dealt with.
Can't ring up and ask for another
cos I can't remember

what on earth it was about.
Except they said it was important.
Must send it by return of post.

Why does death generate
so much paperwork?

Why does it all seem
so unimportant?

Some days I would spend hours just sitting with the cat on my lap, staring into space. It gave me an excuse not to get up and have to decide what to do — the cat wouldn't like being disturbed.

Stroking cats

Stroking cats
is better than eating
chocolate.
    You don't put on weight.

Stroking cats
is better than having
yet another drink.
    You don't get drunk.

Stroking cats
is better than taking
tranquillisers.
    You don't get addicted.

Stroking cats
calms and comforts.
It makes the cat
    feel much better.

Yet again there was an incomprehensible letter from the mortgage company. My mind refused to take it in. I abandoned it in tears and went and put the kettle on.

Absentminded

My mind isn't on the job in hand,
and I do things automatically.
But how silly of me!
I never could stand
salt in my tea.

I found it very difficult to concentrate. I couldn't listen to the radio, watch television or read a book for very long without my attention wandering. I'd also find myself going out of the front door, or from one room to another, and not having the faintest idea why.

Forgetting

No, my mind isn't on the job in hand,
I freely admit it and
frequently I find myself, well,
not where I should be at all.

I've just not been sleeping
so I set off to get a prescription
but instead of going to the doctors
the car went to Tescos.

So I bought the milk I forgot yesterday.

I thought I'd sorted out probate
but there's yet more legal stuff to cope with.
Well, forget the solicitors,
the car went to Tescos.

Wish I hadn't forgotten my mobile.

Tomorrow it's the dentist.
I've been putting it off since last August.
I know I'll be shaking with fright
but with any luck and despite
my very best intentions,
the car will end up in Tescos.

Believe it or not this poem came about after a discussion with my younger daughter about epitaphs for a headstone.

Carpe Diem – Seize the day

For Rachael

A new day is an opportunity not to be missed.
I must make a list.

There are so many things to be done;
first, I'll put the kettle back on.

I need another cup of tea,
just, of course, for energy.

Next, there's that last piece of blackberry tart,
then I really will make a start.

It's not that I'm lazy or slacking;
deep down, I want to get cracking.

I'll get round to things soon,
and seize the afternoon.

I contacted Cruse Bereavement Care and made an appointment to see one of their counsellors, Judy G. It was such a relief to be able to put aside an hour a week to voice my thoughts and feelings – however bizarre and extreme. Judy suggested that I picture my grief as a whirlpool.

Whirlpool

I'm struggling, can't breathe,
dragged down in this vacuum
of being without you,
stopped from drowning
only by hands that reach out to me.

How I yearn for the time
before you died,
drifting contentedly;
no need of other hands
while I had yours.
Now I cling to them.

Slowly, gently, with infinite
patience, I begin to strike out,
one breath at a time, knowing that
when the going gets rough,
hands will be there to steady me.

And now there come increasing
moments of calm water,
of quiet sadness, of reflection,
and a growing sense
of your comforting presence.

In the months that followed Nikki and Robin's deaths, I found that as I gradually stopped feeling shocked and numb, I began to feel even worse, if that were possible. I think this was because all distraction, such as making arrangements and constantly opening the door or answering the telephone, had disappeared, and now I had to fall back on my own resources and try to create a new daily routine.

Loss

What was planned
has had to be unpicked;
dinner out abandoned,
a holiday suddenly lost.

More painful is the slow
unravelling of everyday life.
No-one to put the kettle on,
but myself.

Everywhere I looked there seemed to be a space; the house and also the garden felt so empty. Then there were things I would come across: items of clothing still hanging up, a favourite mug, and above all the absence of familiar objects such as a book – not mine – lying around and the usual muddle of newspapers.

Window

Looking through the window
where the first frosts sit
on the apple tree,

my gaze shifts to the patio
and the old round table,
once white, now grained with age,

and the chairs, some propped against the rain.
The space where you sat is already
six months old.

No newspaper lies discarded,
no mug half-filled with tea.
Your parka hanging on the peg

has shrugged off your shape.
This space where you once were
goes on living,

unlike you,
and occupies another season,
a winter, without you.

Going to look for a book in my younger
daughter's bookcase, I suddenly came
across a photograph of us all walking
along a Norfolk beach, with a wonderful
wintry sunset behind us. All thoughts of
the book went from my head as I was
catapulted back into that happy time. And
then came the shock and realisation yet
again of my loss.

Norfolk sands

For Emma

We walked with the wind at our backs
along the Norfolk sand,
        laughing
we flung pebbles, aimed them far,
counted as they skimmed the sea and sank.

Braving the edge of the waves
we stood there, hair windblown,
        hugging,
happy to be together, needing the close
warmth on that icy, late afternoon.

Under the immense sky, spellbound,
we watched a cormorant diving for fish;
        contented,
we trudged homeward across the wet sand,
our footprints vanishing behind us.

Now the waves ebb and flow
on the winter washed sand
        without you,
and a lone seagull rises
against the pale evening sun.

This photograph of Robin and me stood near the television in the sitting room which I had to go through to get to the kitchen, so I could hardly avoid seeing it. There were other photographs around of course, but it was this particular one, taken not long ago, that seemed to be a focus for my loss.

The Photograph

At first I almost took the photograph
down. It showed the two of us
together, walking in the Chiltern hills.

We had stopped for a rest. I leant
against you, your arm round me,
my head on your shoulder.

The pain I felt each time I saw it
was so acute, it made me feel
again my overwhelming loss.

But to stare at the space it would
leave would be worse. So it
stayed. And gradually as time

passed, I made a friend of pain.
And now, in moments of anxiety,
I stand and look at the photograph.

I lean on you still and will all
my life. Your arm round me.
My head on your shoulder.

Some days I had difficulty putting one foot in front of the other. I had no energy whatsoever. I discovered I was breathing in a very shallow way, sometimes even holding my breath, and I would let out great sighs.

Grief

For Judy G

I must be gentle with myself
at this time,
not beat myself up thinking of
things not done.

For it takes endless patience
to grieve,
and all my energy today
just to breathe.

As a child I would often go out at night and stand on a low wall in our garden and look up at the stars and feel the mystery of it all. Now that two of my children had died, the age-old questions had become very urgent for me: Why were we born? What happens when we die?

Where are you?

Back where the stars start
and the winds begin,
        where were you?

When the sun was born
before the earth burst into being,
        where were you?

As leaves fleshed out bone-thin branches
for a brief while in this world
        you were here.

And as blossom danced in the spinning of
seasons and apples were eaten
        you were here.

Now life has turned through green to gold to
dust and leaves lie on the ground;
        where are you?

And lonely, I watch the winter moon
steal through an eternity of stars;
        where are you?

On days when I had been busier than usual I found that later in the day waves of profound loss would sweep over me. I suppose it was because I got tired and when I'm tired I find it harder to cope. I also discovered I needed to put some time aside during the day just to be still and let the emotions come to the surface.

Silent time

I meet you in the morning
in the silent time

in my chair overlooking the garden,
cradling my cup of tea.

I sit motionless
slow breath after breath,

and in this silent time
sometimes I seem

to merge into the mystery
of it all and feel

your comforting presence flowing
through me and around me.

In the silent time.

The first Christmas I took care to be with friends and relatives, which was a lifesaver. But there were still moments that I felt overwhelmed by loss. In the end I found comfort by lighting a candle. Each Christmas Eve I now go down to the churchyard with my younger daughter and put night lights on the grave where Nikki and Robin are buried. Watching the candles burn in the dark gives me a feeling of inexpressibly deep comfort.

Lighting a candle

I lit a candle for you yesterday.
It seemed a comfort as I sat alone
in the sitting room, a joyous presence,

as if you'd walked in once again
with your wayward humour and listening
heart,
and I sat motionless, held in your love.

Now the candle is cold and I stare
at the unliving wax skin
that once supported the beating flame

and I wonder where you are now.
Are you waiting, stilled and existing
in worlds I know nothing of?

Until that moment
when it is time once again
to light the candle.

I often go for walks through the beech woods in the Chiltern hills. We used to walk there a lot as a family, all five of us. A favourite one is Whiteleaf Cross, another, Lodge Hill. Somehow just putting one foot in front of the other in such beautiful surroundings helps to release my thoughts and emotions.

The beech woods

One day, far
into the future,
I may look back
at this time
and remember, with some
longing, the acute joy
of sun setting through beech trees
and that nearness to you.

I remember writing after Robin's death: 'When you died I felt a moment of extraordinary relief, perhaps because it's all over. I feel extremely guilty about this.' My counsellor reassured me that many people experience these feelings.

Beginnings and endings

The most peaceful time of all is
at the change of things. At dawn
when I watch the night mist

into morning and familiar forms
born back into being.
At sunset when shapes

of day die and silhouettes
of the unknown night
slip around me. When you died

there was a moment's incomparable
peace after the pain of it. But
your being dead is unchanging,

it is all endless. When I die,
it will be for me, perhaps,
the end of memory, certainly the end

of loss. It will be then for others
to mark the mystery
of beginnings and endings.

The most peaceful time of all is
at the change of things.

A friend gave me the book, 'No death, no fear', by the Buddhist monk Thich Nhat Hanh. I found great consolation in its gentle and compassionate wisdom.

Rain

with thanks to Thich Nhat Hanh

Take time
to look at a cloud,
it was not always

above you. Before
it was formed
it was water

in the sea or
perhaps the river.
But it changed,

became vapour, became
the cloud above you
and soon

it will change again,
it will disappear from
your sight. Walk

in the rain, feel
the rain on your face,
look deeply

at the raindrops you hold
in your hands and you will
see the cloud.

Although it is not
as it was, the cloud
is not lost;

in the rain
falling around you
it lives again.

Robin once said to me: 'Whatever happens to you, however earth shattering, however painful, you can still find something, somewhere, that will bring you joy.'

Looking at clouds

Now I have to live
    both our lives,
see things through your eyes
    as well as mine.

So at times, I quell
    my instincts for getting on
and lie on the grass
    and look at clouds.

In the drifting shapes
    I make out a cat
one moment then a clown.
    Begin to smile as you did.

They say those who are gone
    live in the things we do,
so I look at clouds
    because you loved them.

I seemed to spend my time either reliving the past or worrying about what the future would bring. Glancing through a book belonging to a friend of mine I read the words, 'today is all we have; make the most of it'. It hit home.

Autumn leaves

Strange, I have been walking
through the late Autumn lanes
for the past hour, lost
in thought, not noticing

the russet, gold and honey toned leaves
tossing themselves under my feet,
willing me to be part
of it all, and I stopped,

in shock. Is this
how I'm existing – trapped in the past
or buried in fear of the future?
No, I want to be fully present

in each moment of my life,
to stride through beech-wood lanes,
to kick crisp bursts of leaves
into the cold breath of the sunlit air,

and before I become vein thin
with my own winter, to celebrate
this difficult, this painful,
this impossibly beautiful world.

The first year I walked down to a nearby field and picked blackberries from the hedgerow. Day after day I picked blackberries; it felt a safe thing to do.

Picking blackberries

Do you pick blackberries
   at the end
      of summer? Can you
         smell the blackberry

crumble cooking in the oven and
   taste the first
      mouthful
         while your fingers still

prick with thorns and drip
   with dark juice? There is
      nothing so sure
         as the blackberry world which

comes and goes and comes
   again, unlike our
      uneasy world where birth
         doesn't wait for spring, champagne

can be spilt at any time of year
   and dying
      doesn't need a winter.
         What is it that keeps you alive

when you loosen your hold
   on everyday things, when you begin
      to grow invisible
         with all this

loss, all this
   leaving? All
      I know and can tell you is
         that in my shifting world of

unseasonable endings
   I crave the certainty of blackberry things,
      each in its accustomed place,
         and I say a silent thank-you

at the end of another
   summer, when I grasp
      each ripe berry and my fingers are once
         again stained purple.

This might appear a simple poem but my thoughts are actually more complex. I do not know what happens after death; my mind cannot grasp such an immense concept. I am content to wonder and let be what will be. I instinctively feel that all that great love which was in my children, that energy, cannot just have disappeared; it must be somewhere. When I die I will not have to leave them behind. They have gone through the barrier of death before me.

Facing death

I do not fear death,
    or even dying,
        like some do.

For when it comes,
    you will be waiting.
        I will be with you.

There came a point, after a good deal of grieving had been done, when I had to make a choice. Having been flattened by the events in my life, I could either stay prostrate, stuck in the past, or I could pick myself up and give life a chance. It's not been easy, in fact it's been very tough, but each day, step by step and remembering to breathe, I'm still having a go.

Never give up

When the sun fails to shine
on my world,
let me learn to smile.

When the sky thunders
around me,
let me learn to laugh.

And when it all breaks
and the weight of my world
forces me to my knees,
give me courage
to grit my teeth,
haul myself up,
and on the bare
unrelenting earth,
let me learn to dance.

I wrote this poem a long time ago; in fact it is the oldest poem in the collection. I could not believe Nikki had died; the fact was too hard to take in. I also had an overwhelming feeling of guilt. At her service a friend sang the 'Libera me' from Verdi's Requiem. I could not get the music out of my head.

Requiem

Leave me in peace. I shall not stay
with mourners hymning their remembrance.
My song still sings in the beech-wood
wandering hills
and fills the air with laughter,
while you lie silent in pious peace,
in that dark cold hollow
where I cannot find you,
cannot follow.

Leave me in peace. I shall not stay
in this place where they have taken you,
where daffodils trumpet Spring
and grass chokes the earth in a sprawl of
useless life
while you lie lifeless,
trapped in eternal rest,
in that dark, cold hollow
where I cannot find you,
cannot follow.

Leave me in peace. I have to stay
in this world where the moon knells shadows
all around and the wind is out of tune.
But when the beat of my life weakens
and runs out of time,
when melody heals to a murmur
and my song is sung,
then, in that dark, cold hollow,
I shall find you,
I shall follow;
our final requiem.

I spent the first summer after Robin died – it was a good one that year – sitting in the garden, stunned. Now and again I would get up and do a little weeding or put out some bird seed. Any decision exhausted me. I took to watching the birds come and go, always conscious of the sun and wind on my face. I still grieve in my garden; it gives me great comfort.

I am there

I am the breath of wind on your face.
Whether head held high you tread
the hard-edged crags of grief,
or stooped and worn weary out
the windings and unwindings of the day
with each barely breathed sigh you take,
let my touch lift you,
let me be with you.
I am the breath of wind on your face.

I am the sound of birdsong in your garden.
When stumbling
you work the weeds blindly,
or numbed by memories
you slump bone limp in the waiting chair,
I am there, listen to me,
I am singing to you.
I am the sound of birdsong all around.

I am the dawn of the new day;
the light that breaks your unsleeping.
Rise with me, walk with me.
I am there in the mists of the morning
and the change and the change of the seasons.
In the rain on the wind
and the warmth of the waking sun
I am there, lean on me,
I will hold you,
I will always be with you.
I am the dawn of the new day.

An extract from my diary reads: 'I came down early one spring morning and went out into the garden. A robin flew down onto a nearby branch. I stood there with the warmth of the sun on my face and in the stillness I began to feel your presence all around me, even flowing in me and through me. It was a moment of incomparable peace.'

Always

I am still with you,
I am in your hands,
I am in you,
I am you.
Be still, there is
no coming or going,
only being,
and being with you
always.

'Gina Claye's poems explore the strong emotions experienced by those who grieve – feelings that can leave people very isolated. As a bereavement support worker with Cruse, when someone shares a feeling with me which is reflected in one of these poems, I give them that poem to read. They find comfort in knowing they are not alone in their struggle to live with such painful and overwhelming emotions. It takes courage to grieve, and these poems make one very aware of that.'

Judy G
Cruse Bereavement Care

Printed in the United Kingdom
by Lightning Source UK Ltd.
110472UKS00001B/52-102